GETTING MISS Muffet off Her Tuffet

By Susan Sherwood Parr

WORD PRODUCTIONS

GETTING MISS Muffet off Her Tuffet

Word Productions LLC
www.wordproductions.org
Albuquerque, NM 87192 USA

The Go Girl Series:
Getting Miss Muffet Off Her Tuffet
by Susan Sherwood Parr

Back cover photo:
Mike Trompak: TIMELESS IMAGES PHOTOGRAPHY
www.timelessimagesphotography.net

Library of Congress Catalog Card Number Pending
ISBN 978-0-9827998-0-2

Contents

SPECIAL THANKS...

TO PAULA RILEY...

For her exceptional tips to help us all organize our surroundings without getting depressed thinking about it. Paula, you're the best!

TO NATHAN MOSES...

For his contribution to help us learn to watch our attitudes and our bodies nutritional needs. Nathan, thanks for taking the time!

CHAPTER ONE

Get A Lift

GET UP

Little Miss Muffet sat on her tuffet
Eating her curds and whey...

Girls, this book is for those of us who have been tired, lethargic, lost our get-up-and-go. It's for those who are discouraged and for those who may even have physical reasons for needing strength and energy.

We're going to look at all of those aspects when considering solutions for our lives.

Wherefore seeing we also are compassed about with so great a cloud of witnesses, let us lay aside every weight, and the sin which doth so easily beset us, and let us run with patience the race that is set before us, looking unto Jesus the author and finisher of our faith; who for the joy that was set before him endured the cross, despising the

1

shame, and is set down at the right hand of the throne of God. For consider him that endured such contradiction of sinners against himself, lest ye be wearied and faint in your minds. (Hebrews 12:1-3)

Wherever you are in your life, you are on a journey. When Jesus Christ comes into your life the journey becomes sure. Yet, even though God has made provision for all of us, we all face cracks, diversions, and distractions in our lives.

God has provided us with the Redemptive work of Christ, who is the more-than-enough work through which God is able to meet our every need. Look at this exciting verse:

In Him we have redemption through His blood, the forgiveness of sins, according to the riches of His grace which He made to abound toward us in all wisdom and prudence, having made known to us the mystery of His will, according to His good pleasure which He purposed in Himself, that in the dispensation of the fullness of the times He might gather together in one all things in Christ, both which are in heaven and which are on earth—in Him. (Ephesians 1:7-10)

So what is the first thing we do when we need a lift...a lift off our tuffet?

Below in the space provided, I want you to write down your feelings, and/or what you need help with. It may be emotional, spiritual, or physical. Write them down, and we will be taking it all to God together.

The Soap Opera

- I am tired.

- I have no get-up-and-go.

- I don't have enough desire to "do."

- What is wrong with me?

What Do I Want to Pray About?

_____

_____

_____

_____

_____

Take Action

1. Decide to get encouraged—but don't guess at the problem.

2. Consider your life, routine, and health.

3. Realize that God is able to help things and change us.

4. Think: Prayer + Grace= Solutions!

Check Out These Verses on Diligence

You need to fill yourself and surround yourself with a Word of God atmosphere. You will be amazed at the supernatural power within His Word. I know that this is true. In 1 Thessalonians 2:13 it says that His Word 'works effectually in them that believe.' That is so awesome. So let's start now. Let's think about the following:

In all labor there is profit, but idle chatter leads only to poverty. (Proverbs 14:23)

Laziness casts one into a deep sleep, and an idle person will suffer hunger. (Proverbs 19:15)

The soul of a lazy man desires, and has nothing; but the soul of the diligent shall be made rich. (Proverbs 13:4)

The way of the lazy man is like a hedge of thorns, but the way of the upright is a highway. (Proverbs 15:19)

Keep your heart with all diligence, for out of it spring the issues of life. (Proverbs 4:23)

He who has a slack hand becomes poor, but the hand of the diligent makes rich. (Proverbs 10:4)

The hand of the diligent will rule, But the lazy man will be put to forced labor. (Proverbs 12:24)

The lazy man does not roast what he took in hunting, but diligence is man's precious possession. (Proverbs 13:4)

The soul of a lazy man desires, and has nothing; but the soul of the diligent shall be made rich. (Proverbs 12:27)

The plans of the diligent lead surely to plenty, but those of everyone who is hasty, surely to poverty. (Proverbs 21:5)

Be diligent to present yourself approved to God, a worker who does not need to be ashamed, rightly dividing the word of truth. (2 Timothy 2:15)

Let us therefore be diligent to enter that rest, lest anyone fall according to the same example of disobedience. (Hebrews 4:11)

And we desire that each one of you show the same diligence to the full assurance of hope until the end. (Hebrews 6:1)

...That you do not become sluggish, but imitate those who through faith and patience inherit the promises. (Hebrews 6:12)

But also for this very reason, giving all diligence, add to your faith virtue, to virtue knowledge. (2 Peter 1:5)

The Cure

The first step for you to take in any situation is to examine your spiritual wellbeing. In this book I will address accepting Jesus Christ as your Lord and Savior, the issue of forgiveness, and add a mini Prayer Workshop that will teach you how to pray scripturally.

1   First, we will all do a bit of self-examination.

2.   Second, let's pray and make sure Jesus Christ is the Lord and Savior of your life:

Jesus, forgive me of all my sins. I believe that You died on the cross for my sins and rose again from the dead. Come inside of my heart, into the very depths of my being through Your Holy Spirit, right now. I make You the Lord and Savior of my life. Take control of my life, and make me into the person you want me to be. Amen. (John 3:16; Romans 10:9-10)

Years ago, someone mailed me a Campus Crusade for Christ Four Spiritual Laws booklet. I skeptically read it, prayed the prayer similar to the one above very critically...then "something [the grace of God] made me pray it a second time...with feeling. It was the Grace of God:

5

For by grace you have been saved through faith, and that not of yourselves; it is the gift of God, not of works, lest anyone should boast. (Ephesians 2:8-9)

3. Third, you need to keep an open mind, moving forward to a new start! The Scripture below proves that you can have a NEW start. By the way, "new creation" in the Greek indicates a new species:

   Therefore, if anyone is in Christ, he is a new creation; old things have passed away; behold, all things have become new. (2 Corinthians 5:17)

Miss Muffet's Workbench

Take heart. God has a plan for you; He has a plan to help you and take care of you. Did you know that the Bible says He has foreordained steps for you to walk in? That was one of the most exciting things I heard when I prayed to ask Christ into my heart and life and to take control! The verse is found in Ephesians 2:10:

For we are His workmanship, created in Christ Jesus for good works, which God prepared beforehand that we should walk in them.

What's My Part?

Now that you are IN CHRIST and we've made sure you are born again, you are ready.

A note to bear in mind: You've been forgiven—make sure you are willing to forgive as well.

1. Stop thinking "I can't."

2. Decide to change

3. Enlarge your view of God—not of yourself.

4. Endeavor to remove all mental blocks to the thought of God changing your life.

What's God's Part?

God cares about everything that has to do with YOU. He loves you. He loves me.

> *Life is more than food, and the body is more than clothing. Consider the ravens, for they neither sow nor reap, which have neither storehouse nor barn; and God feeds them. Of how much more value are you than the birds? And which of you by worrying can add one cubit to his stature?* (Luke 12:23-25)

His promises are true and they belong to all of us in Christ (2 Corinthians 1:20). His Word is true (Romans 3:4). God's Word will accomplish what it purposes to do (Isaiah 55:11).

In light of that knowledge, let's agree that God can help any of us with anything.

So, if you are tired, bored, passive, discouraged, lazy, or if there are physical or emotional problems, God is bigger. No matter what's going on, if -you can't get up and get going, God has an answer and God has more than enough to meet your needs.

Note that in the following verse, Paul the apostle said Jesus would meet ALL our needs, *all...*according to HIS riches in glory by Christ Jesus:

And my God shall supply all your need according to His riches in glory by Christ Jesus. (Philippians 4:19)

"ALL" means *everything* and "His riches by Christ Jesus" means *that because of the redemptive work of the cross, a more-than-enough work, God is limitless in His power toward us.* Limitless! That's great news. So, don't doubt for a moment.

The Prayer

Dear Father, Have mercy on me and forgive me of all of my sins. Please look upon me in my inabilities and my health concerns and help me. I cannot change myself, and only by Your grace can I do what you empower me to do. I give my whole life into Your hands. Please move in my life to help me get up and get going. Grant me healing where needed, in Jesus' name. Amen.

Think About It

Read Chapter 7, Get the Antidote. Here you will find out how to pray and see results. This short chapter will change your life and help you in the rest of the book.

In the upcoming chapters we will touch on many areas with the hope and idea that it will be fun. Let's do this together and let's:

...Look — at God.

...Look — to God's Word the Bible.

...Look — at what God can do.

...Look — to the Lord for His grace to do it.

Remember

For all the promises of God in Him are Yes, and in Him Amen, to the glory of God through us.
(2 Corinthians 1:20)

Certainly not! Indeed, let God be true but every man a liar. As it is written: 'That You may be justified in Your words, and may overcome when You are judged.'
(Romans 3:4)

God's Word will accomplish what it purposes to do:

So shall My word be that goes forth from My mouth; it shall not return to Me void, but it shall accomplish what I please, and it shall prosper in the thing for which I sent it. (Isaiah 55:11)

Promises to Cherish

Therefore, if anyone is in Christ, he is a new creation; old things have passed away; behold, all things have become new. (2 Corinthians 5:17)

And my God shall supply all your need according to His riches in glory by Christ Jesus. (Philippians 4:19)

Then they cried out to the LORD in their trouble, and He saved them out of their distresses. He sent His word and healed them, and delivered them from their destructions. Oh, that men would give thanks to the LORD for His goodness, and for His wonderful works to the children of men! (Psalm 107:19-21)

God is our refuge and strength, A very present help in trouble. Therefore we will not fear, even though the earth be removed, and though the mountains be carried into the midst of the sea; though its waters roar and be troubled, though the mountains shake with its swelling. Selah (Psalm 46:1-3)

Be anxious for nothing, but in everything by prayer and supplication, with thanksgiving, let your requests be made known to God; and the peace of God, which surpasses all understanding, will guard your hearts and minds through Christ Jesus. (Philippians 4:6–7)

For this reason I bow my knees to the Father of our Lord Jesus Christ, from whom the whole family in heaven and earth is named, that He would grant you, according to the riches of His glory, to be strengthened with might through His Spirit in the inner man, that Christ may dwell in your hearts through faith; that you, being rooted and grounded in love, may be able to comprehend with all the saints what is the width and length and depth and height—to know the love of Christ which passes knowledge; that you may be filled with all the fullness of God. Now to Him who is able to do exceedingly abundantly above all that we ask or think, according to the power that works in us, to Him be glory in the church by Christ Jesus to all generations, forever and ever. Amen (Ephesians 3:14-21)

If you abide in Me, and My words abide in you, you will ask what you desire, and it shall be done for you. (John 15:7)

This Book of the Law shall not depart from your mouth, but you shall meditate in it day and night, that you may observe to do according to all that is written in it. For then you will make your way prosperous, and then you will have good success. (Joshua 1:8)

Today's Date_____

My Prayers

_____
_____
_____
_____
_____
_____
_____
_____
_____
_____
_____
_____
_____
_____
_____
_____
_____
_____
_____
_____
_____
_____
_____
_____
_____
_____

*Today's Date*_____

My Answers

_____
_____
_____
_____
_____
_____
_____
_____
_____
_____
_____
_____
_____
_____
_____
_____
_____
_____
_____
_____
_____
_____
_____
_____
_____

*Today's Date*_____

My Thoughts

_____

_____

_____

_____

_____

_____

_____

_____

_____

_____

_____

_____

_____

_____

_____

_____

_____

_____

_____

_____

_____

_____

_____

_____

_____

CHAPTER TWO

Get Vision

LOSE THE LIMIT

Get a new vision! Go ahead. Just think about looking away from your tiredness, lethargy, and faults. Get distracted from your needs. Get distracted from yourself. Look at God. Today you woke up and it was a new morning. We can forget yesterday. In fact, it is best that we do. Good memories can come, but for now let's think about *newness*. Let's all get a new view with a larger expanse. Remember, we are not looking at what you can do. We are looking to God almighty.

Read this verse and think about how you could have been limiting God in your need:

> *Do not remember the former things, nor consider the things of old. Behold, I will do a new thing, now it shall spring forth; shall you not know it? I will even make a road in the wilderness and rivers in the desert.* (Isaiah 43:18-19)

God is the God of new things. He is a creator. If you ask Him, there are no limits to what He can do. So let's start today with a new vision; new sight. This time, let's remove all limits:

Enlarge the place of your tent, and let them stretch out the curtains of your dwellings; do not spare; lengthen your cords, and strengthen your stakes. For you shall expand to the right and to the left, and your descendants will inherit the nations, and make the desolate cities inhabited. (Isaiah 54:2-3)

The Soap Opera

- I don't want to do anything.
- I feel tired; I have no energy.
- I am often without emotion.
- I'm bored.

What Do I Want to Pray About?

_____

_____

_____

_____

_____

Take Action

1. Today is a new day.
2. Next, look at God's horizon. Think: It has no end.
3. Now, think about God's power.
4. And lastly, think about His grace and how He cares for your every need.

The Cure

Girls, today is a brand new day. Today is a day of new vision; a day of looking at Jesus Christ and not at ourselves. Let's look at Jesus Christ who can do *anything.* He loves you.

Get vision. Get His vision. His vision is His will for you. His will for you is that you receive the grace to help in time of need. In Him as your sufficiency.

Get Perspective. We are going to pray and also look at what we can do naturally to receive help.

Ask yourself these questions: What if I have let my health slip? What if my nutrition or habits have played a part in how I feel?

Miss Muffet's Workbench

What's My Part?

1. Spend some time with God. Spend time as though He were right there having a cup of tea or coffee with you. Sit with Him. It is not hard. Look at this:

    My soul, wait silently for God alone, for my expectation is from Him. He only is my rock and my salvation; He is my defense; I shall not be moved. (Psalm 62:5-6)

2. When you look at God and His Word, you are looking at a solution. God is interested in every detail of your life. Now we can confidently know you are getting somewhere. If you don't have it already, you will definitely get NEW

VISION. What better place for your eyes and heart to be but on God and His Word and HIS strength and power? You want to have God's perspective. You are on your way!

3. Remember, you are going to pray about everything. God will hear your prayers.

God's Part

God will hear you and answer your prayers:

Now this is the confidence that we have in Him, that if we ask anything according to His will, He hears us. And if we know that He hears us, whatever we ask, we know that we have the petitions that we have asked of Him. (1 John 5:14–15)

His promises are yours. God will do what He says He will do:

For all the promises of God in Him are Yes, and in Him Amen, to the glory of God through us. (2 Corinthians 1:20)

The Prayer

Dear heavenly Father, I can't change myself, and I ask for Your grace, and help, enthusiasm, and for more energy. Your Word says if I ask anything according to Your will, You hear me and I have it (1 John 5:14). It also says that whatever I ask in Jesus name, you will give me (John 13:14). Father, I ask for all these things in Jesus' name. I rest my faith in Your integrity and in the integrity of Your holy Word (Numbers 23:19)

Think About It

You have asked the Creator of the universe for help.

...God created you.
...God can help you.
...God can give vision.

Promises to Cherish

[God] remembered us in our lowly state, for His mercy endures forever. (Psalm 136:23)

Though the LORD is on high, yet He regards the lowly; but the proud He knows from afar. (Psalm 138:6)

Better to be of a humble spirit with the lowly, than to divide the spoil with the proud. (Proverbs16:19)

The LORD is near to those who have a broken heart, and saves such as have a contrite spirit. (Psalm 34:18)

The sacrifices of God are a broken spirit, a broken and a contrite heart—these, O God, You will not despise. (Psalm 51:17)

"For all those things My hand has made, and all those things exist," says the LORD. "But on this one will I look: on him who is poor and of a contrite spirit, and who trembles at My word." (Isaiah 66:2)

*Today's Date*_____

My Prayers

_____
_____
_____
_____
_____
_____
_____
_____
_____
_____
_____
_____
_____
_____
_____
_____
_____
_____
_____
_____
_____
_____
_____

*Today's Date*_____

My Answers

_____
_____
_____
_____
_____
_____
_____
_____
_____
_____
_____
_____
_____
_____
_____
_____
_____
_____
_____
_____
_____
_____
_____
_____
_____

Today's Date_____

My Thoughts

_____
_____
_____
_____
_____
_____
_____
_____
_____
_____
_____
_____
_____
_____
_____
_____
_____
_____
_____
_____
_____
_____
_____

CHAPTER THREE

Get Energy

TOSS THE TUFFET!

If any of you lacks wisdom, let him ask of God, who gives to all liberally and without reproach, and it will be given to him. (James 1:5)

…Nutrition?
    …Contrition?
        …Ambition?

Well, what is it? What has been the problem? Could it be nutrition? Does your spiritual health need a boost? And do you lack the energy to investigate it all? Well, we're going to go there.

This chapter contains some tips and nutritional facts to help you be your own detective. You can make a checklist to help you decide the underlying cause and to do something about it all.

The Soap Opera

- I don't know what's wrong.
- I've thought about "reasons."
- I'm curious about new thinking.
- I'd like to hear more.

What Do I Want to Pray About?

_____

_____

_____

_____

_____

Take Action

1. I'm going to read the points to consider.
2. I will consider the possibilities.
3. I will first realize I don't do anything on my own.
4. Realize God can do anything.

The Cure

Get Joy. Enjoy what you are doing. Enjoy considering God, His Word, the nutrition facts you may not have heard about. [Note that these are not a prescription or medical advice, but just a friend's research; sharing it with us.]

Get Openness. Realize you don't know everything. Let God do a new work on the inside of you.

Get Hope. Just pray about it. Did you know you can sit down and visit with the Lord like a best friend? There are scriptures that confirm He says to wait before Him...even silently. So if you are concerned about running out of words to pray or say...forget it! Enjoy time with God.

Next Steps

Now you are ready for the next step. You have stopped to consider God in your situation, you have prayed about it, and you have asked God's grace to help.

He heard you. His Word says He hears you. Okay girls, let's toss the tuffet! Let's get up and get going.

> *Trust in the LORD with all your heart, and lean not on your own understanding; in all your ways acknowledge Him, and He shall direct your paths.* (Proverbs 3:3–5)

Meet Nathan Moses...A Look At Nutrition

Nathaniel Moses graduated from the University of New Mexico with a degree in Business Communications and Psychology. He began working in the family business, Moses Kountry Health Food Store [www.moseshealth.com], when he was 13 years of age. He now runs the business full time.

He is actively involved in a local church and in ministry and has been a national television guest on Sky Angel.

I've asked Nathan for just a few nuggets of advice; and what info he might know about that would help problems like lethargy, listlessness, tiredness, etc.

Moses Says...

If you are tired all the time it may be because you have Chronic Fatigue Syndrome. I'm finding this may be the case because you've had to take a lot of antibiotics. Here are a few useful tips that cover several areas:

- Replacing the beneficial bacteria with probiotics can be helpful; doing a yeast cleanse may also be helpful.

- Replacing caffeine in the diet with B-Vitamins is another bit of advice. Caffeine releases adrenaline and after a while will wear out the adrenal glands. By mid-afternoon your adrenal glands give out and your energy levels crash. Holy basil assists with adrenal fatigue as well.

- Ginseng increases circulation without being a stimulant like caffeine.

- Also, when people tell me they need energy I ask them how they are sleeping. Typically they aren't sleeping very well.

- I would recommend not taking any stimulants any time past noon, as stimulants can stay in your liver for a long time. Stimulants include caffeine, chocolate, and peppers, and even salt and pepper.

- There are several herbs that help with sleep as well as taking some melatonin. Once you get some restful sleep you'll wake up with more energy.

- Also there are supplements if people aren't sleeping due to emotional issues.

Past the nutritional bit of advice, Moses says this about your attitude:

"Let someone else take care of it. Let someone else give their money, their time and their talent." Ever heard that? Scripture says: *"Let each man give according as he has determined in his heart; not grudgingly, or under compulsion; for God loves a cheerful giver."* (2 Corinthians 9:7)

Being proactive rather than being reactive? Reactive is the lazy way out. Taking a little preventative medicine can help you avoid having to clean up an even bigger mess later.

What's cheaper, taking food supplements that could potentially prevent a heart attack, or having open heart surgery? Also, another way of saying it is "doing what's right instead of what's most convenient or cheaper." You could hire a plumber that's cheaper, but when your bath tub starts to leak and falls through the floor how much is that going to cost?

Toss That Tuffet!

You've tossed the tuffet. You're running the race that Christ has set before you:

Do you not know that those who run in a race all run, but one receives the prize? Run in such a way that you may obtain it. And everyone who competes for the prize is temperate in all things. Now they do it to obtain a perishable crown, but we for an imperishable crown. (1 Corinthians 9:24)

Element for Change

There is one more critical element to consider in the adventure of getting up and getting going!

In my book, *7 Steps Out of the Humpty Dumps,* God had shown me how critical it is to help someone else and get involved in your church. When we help others in any way, God is using our hands. We can be the 'hands and feet of Jesus' to someone else in need. Helping others is like a lifeblood to our spiritual, emotional, and ultimately physical health.

Re-evaluate involvement in your church, considering how you can become involved if your not. Remember, we are not an island, but we live with other people; we are families; we are the body of Christ and members in particular.

Miss Muffet's Workbench

Spend some time in God's Word each day. Have a visit with the Lord. Tell Him what is going on. Remember, He is your Creator, your Friend, and your everything. Sit with the Lord and just relax in His presence. Thank God for what He is doing in your life. Thank Him for what He is doing for others who are in need. Stay in His presence until He gives you a measure of comfort and peace for yourself, and for all you are praying about.

Get Glasses

By praying scripturally and resting in His Word and thanking Him for what He will do according to His will, God's grace will enter into your life. God is more than able to give us all new vision for our lives. Pray for vision…His vision. We want to see and think what He wants us to see and think.

What Is My Part?

You need to…

- Look at the facts.
- Get glasses that help you see [grace].
- Consider the Scriptures; nutrition facts; other possibilities.
- Pray about it.

What Is God's Part?

God is working mightily in you. His Word is at work within you. It works. It is God!
His Word says:

> *It is God who works in you both to will and to do for His good pleasure.* (Philippians 2:13)

> *For this reason we also thank God without ceasing, because when you received the word of God which you heard from us, you welcomed it not as the word of men, but as it is in truth, the word of God, which also effectively works in you who believe.* (1 Thessalonians 2:13)

The Prayer

Dear God, I ask You to work inside of my heart, mind, soul, spirit, and body. Make me into what You want me to be. Regenerate my life. I want to be what you want, but realize that without you I am nothing. Please work inside of me. Please let your Word work mightily in me, in Jesus' name.

Think About It

God is your God.

God loves you.

God knows everything, and everything you need.

God will answer your prayers.

Let's all move forward. Let's do it together. Make your decision while reading this book to bring all to the Lord. Let's start with prayer.

Promises to Cherish

But we all, with unveiled face, beholding as in a mirror the glory of the Lord, are being transformed into the same image from glory to glory, just as by the Spirit of the Lord. (2 Corinthians 3:18)

Better to be of a humble spirit with the lowly, than to divide the spoil with the proud. (Proverbs 16:19)

In Him also we have obtained an inheritance, being predestined according to the purpose of Him who works all things according to the counsel of His will, that we who first trusted in Christ should be to the praise of His glory. (Ephesians 1:11–12)

Therefore we also, since we are surrounded by so great a cloud of witnesses, let us lay aside every weight, and the sin which so easily ensnares us, and let us run with endurance the race that is set before us, looking unto Jesus, the author and finisher of our faith, who for the joy that was set before Him endured the cross, despising the shame, and has sat down at the right hand of the throne of God. (Hebrews 12:1-3)

But if any of you lacks wisdom, let him ask of God, who gives to all generously and without reproach, and it will be given to him. (James 1:5)

*Today's Date*_____

My Prayers

_____
_____
_____
_____
_____
_____
_____
_____
_____
_____
_____
_____
_____
_____
_____
_____
_____
_____
_____
_____
_____
_____
_____
_____

Today's Date_____

My Answers

_____
_____
_____
_____
_____
_____
_____
_____
_____
_____
_____
_____
_____
_____
_____
_____
_____
_____
_____
_____
_____
_____
_____
_____
_____
_____

*Today's Date*_____

My Thoughts

_____
_____
_____
_____
_____
_____
_____
_____
_____
_____
_____
_____
_____
_____
_____
_____
_____
_____
_____
_____
_____
_____
_____
_____
_____

CHAPTER FOUR

Get Sense

GET OFF THE FENCE

Where will you go, Miss Muffet? Will you choose the way of the Lord? You have chosen the Lord as your God. Here is what He promises as you GET GOING:

And though the Lord gives you the bread of adversity and the water of affliction, yet your teachers will not be moved into a corner anymore, but your eyes shall see your teachers. Your ears shall hear a word behind you, saying, "This is the way, walk in it," whenever you turn to the right hand or whenever you turn to the left... (Isaiah 30:20-21)

I will lay waste the mountains and hills, and dry up all their vegetation; I will make the rivers coastlands, and I will dry up the pools. I will bring the blind by a way they did not know; I will lead them in paths they have not known. I will make darkness light before them, and

*crooked places straight. These things I will do for them,
and not forsake them.* (Isaiah 42:15-16)

And one more marvelous verse that confirms that God's desire
is to lead you and that He can actually lead you:

*For if you live according to the flesh you will die; but if
by the Spirit you put to death the deeds of the body, you
will live. For as many as are led by the Spirit of God,
these are sons of God. For you did not receive the spirit
of bondage again to fear, but you received the Spirit of
adoption by whom we cry out, "Abba, Father."*
(Romans 8:13-15)

Meet Miss Organization

I realize that all is not spiritual, and that we all have natural,
physical, and nutritional needs. I'm going to introduce a friend
of mine to you! Her name is Paula Riley. She is going to help
us all in this chapter. She has a gift. In addition to teaching
God's Word, Paula has given workshops for women regarding
organization. But first, a bit more about Paula. Here is what
Paula has to say about herself:

*My name is Paula Riley, a wife and a mother. Organiza-
tion came pretty easy for me because I grew up in a very
clean and organized house. However when I became a
mom, I found myself overwhelmed and the piles getting
bigger! I took charge one day so that I could enjoy my
family more. When I have a passion in life, I usually
tackle it head-on and sometimes it works and sometimes
it doesn't. I'm very involved in my kids' activities as a
team mom and cheerleader, I love my kids. I am also a
Pastor's wife so I spend a lot of time encouraging my*

36

*wonderful husband and coming alongside him to keep
our family strong and healthy. I love to serve others
makes me feel happy and blessed.*

Encouraging Words from Paula...

Organization is something we all put on the "back burner." We
all say, "Oh, I'll get to it later." The problem is we never do, and
things pile up and before we know it, it seems like we will never
dig ourselves out of the huge mess we've created!

Well I'm here to tell you that it is possible for anyone to
become organized! It just takes a little time and patience, and
you are on your way to a stress-free, organized, tidy house.

Set Some Goals

I encourage you to start by setting small goals and doing projects one at a time. Otherwise you will become overwhelmed
and eventually quit. When the first goal is finished, you will be
proud of yourself, that you persevered and finished well, and
the end result: Freedom! Don't forget: have fun! This is all to
make your life easier and to enable you to enjoy the other
things you love, without having to stress about what's waiting
for you at home.

One last thing, I highly recommend that you get your family
involved, especially the kids. They will feel ownership of their
tidy and organized rooms. I promise you they will want to
keep it that way! When getting organized becomes a team
effort, the possibilities are endless! Have fun!

Paula's Quick Steps Toward Getting Organized

1. **Start one project at a time.** Make sure it is small; you don't want to make it a goal that is too large and makes you want to quit.

2. **Purge!** Throw things away you don't need or use rarely. If it's something in good shape, you can donate it to a youth missions trip garage sale or shelter.

3. **Purchase baskets or containers.** These are things that will make your life easier as you put items in them and label what is inside for easy access. For instance: start with a food pantry and wicker baskets. This saved me from chaos!

4. **Don't spend a lot of money!** You can find storage containers at dollar or discount stores that don't break your wallet. They work just as well! Getting organized doesn't have to cost a lot.

5. **Have Fun!** The end result from your project is *worth it!*

The Soap Opera

- I don't have the power I need.
- I need help to get started.
- I would like some help.
- I need encouragement.

What Do I Want to Pray About?

_____

_____

_____

_____

_____

Take Action

1. Now that you are beginning to get some encouragement and benefit from the experience of others, you can have hope for the future.

2. God is your help. He has sent His Spirit to help, comfort, lead, guide…

3. Toss the previous "I can't." Instead,pray about it.

4. Look to God's grace for all. See how the Lord will begin to help you.

The Cure

Decide that with God's grace, you will get into the mode of trusting God to make the changes.

You will receive the power of the Holy Spirit needed for *your* situation.

You will be able to share what God has done for you with someone else.

>…Go somewhere
>…Get nutrition
>…Get active
>…Get started

It is God who works in you both to will and to do of His good pleasure. (Philippians 2:13)

Miss Muffet's Workbench

God does the work. Who ever said you had to do it? He can recreate us all from the inside out. He has GRACE. The reliability of God's Word proves He will answer your prayers. You have not prayed some ridiculous or selfish prayer. You have prayed for a positive life and health change toward His will for your life.

What Is My Part?

1. **Write your goals down.** There is a lot of research which has shown that writing them down helps them to be reached. I would say write them on your prayer list. Of course, they need to be realistic and in God's will. My greatest joy has been when I have seen God bring things to pass that I have prayed about.

2. **Consider your vision.** Determine to enlarge it by not limiting God.

3. Remember to pray and spend time with the Lord each day. Look in the back of the book at the prayer section. These keys are valuable and will show you how to pray scripturally, thanking God for what He is doing and will do according to His will.

What Is God's Part?

There is nothing too hard for God. He delights in relationship with you and in answering your prayers. Look at these verses:

For I know the thoughts that I think toward you, says the LORD, thoughts of peace and not of evil, to give you a future and a hope. (Jeremiah 29:11)

The Prayer

Dear God, please lead and guide me in this new journey. Help me make reasonable goals. Grant me the energy, enthusiasm I desire in your work in me. Help me be contagious in the joy of the Lord. Thank you for this new life, in Jesus' name. Amen.

Think About It

Be content and happy that you have prayed about everything. That is so awesome. Who better to take your troubles to? Who better to communicate with and share your deepest heart's desires with than with your Lord? He loves it too! You are in a good place.

Promises to Cherish

If you then, being evil, know how to give good gifts to your children, how much more will your Father who is in heaven give good things to those who ask Him. (Matt. 7:11)

Jesus said to him, "If you want to be perfect, go, sell what you have and give to the poor, and you will have treasure in heaven; and come, follow Me. (Matt. 19:21)

He who finds his life will lose it, and he who loses his life for My sake will find it. (Matt. 10:39)

Today's Date_____

My Prayers

_____
_____
_____
_____
_____
_____
_____
_____
_____
_____
_____
_____
_____
_____
_____
_____
_____
_____
_____
_____
_____
_____
_____
_____
_____
_____
_____
_____
_____

My Answers

_____

_____

_____

_____

_____

_____

_____

_____

_____

_____

_____

_____

_____

_____

_____

_____

_____

_____

_____

_____

_____

_____

_____

_____

_____

Today's Date_____

My Thoughts

_____
_____
_____
_____
_____
_____
_____
_____
_____
_____
_____
_____
_____
_____
_____
_____
_____
_____
_____
_____
_____
_____
_____

CHAPTER FIVE

Get the Keys

MISS MUFFET

There are Four Keys to a Close Walk with God. What are they? They will help you understand yourself and what God wants you to do. Be determined to get going, to look forward, and walk into the opportunities available. Implementing these keys will change your life. God knows we need each other. God knows you need to be around others to give, share, and care. He also knows you need to be cared about.

Wow! That said it all. It's the truth. It really Isaiah While God can help us in so many wonderful ways, you can make some plans!

The Soap Opera

- I am not sure I can do this
- I am concerned I will forget to pray.
- I have felt like giving up.

What Do I Want to Pray About?

_____

_____

_____

_____

_____

Take Action

1. Refuse to worry about anything. Confess worry, because it is sin. Did you know that? If you are really trusting in a loving, caring God and have given Him your all, why should you worry?

2. Pray in detail about everything. This will bring great peace to your heart and mind.

3. Put Philippians 4:6–7 into practice. It works. You can pray this way: "Father, speak to so-and-so, and move on them by Your Spirit. And Lord, please, if it be Your will, turn such-and-such situation around, in Jesus' name."

4. Trust in God, His integrity, the integrity of His Word, and His promises. Do not trust in yourself. Thank God and praise Him for what He is doing according to His will.

The Cure

Resting and counting on God's integrity, the integrity of His Word and promises, is the best thing you can do. Learning how to approach God and then seeing results is an exciting thing. Be determined to:

...receive God's grace.

...pray in detail.

...stand on the promises in the Bible.

...thank Him for all He has done and is going to do.

...receive God's peace after I pray.

Miss Muffet's Workbench

Let God do a new thing in your life. Give Him a chance to move by His grace and Spirit. He has foreordained steps for you to walk in.

What Is My Part?

1. Put Key One into practice. There's no time like the present. Adjust your schedule. Put God and His Word first in your life.

2. Enlarge your life. Find Christian friends; find healthy places to go and clean, fun things to do. Put Key Two into practice.

3. Reassess your physical health. Our bodies are the temples of the Holy Spirit. Remember that you need proper nutrition and exercise. That is Key Three.

4. Get involved. This will rid you of that stagnant feeling. You will become spiritually healthy and happy when you get involved and give of yourself in some way. That's Key Four.

5. Pray about these aspects of your life. Thank God and praise Him for what He is doing and is going to do in your life.

What Is God's Part?

God cares about every aspect of our lives and wants us to draw near to Him. He responds to our prayers.

1. The next time you spend time with the Lord, make it a point to sit quietly before Him. Give Him a chance to speak to you.

   Call to Me, and I will answer you, and show you great and mighty things, which you do not know. (Jeremiah 33:3)

   In the day of my trouble I will call upon You, for You will answer me. (Psalm 86:7)

2. Remember—God hears you, loves you, and will answer you. It doesn't matter if at times you don't see answers immediately. God is at work!

   As you do not know what is the way of the wind, or how the bones grow in the womb of her who is with child, so you do not know the works of God who makes everything. (Ecclesiastes 11:5)

The Prayer

Dear Lord, I want to be energized and walk in full freedom. I want to be free to walk in all that you desire for my life. I want to love You more and feel loved by You. Thank you for what you have been doing in my life. Thank you for wisdom and tools to grow spiritually and physically. Thank you for giving me this strength and wisdom, in Jesus' name.

Think About it

- Do the Four Keys to a Close Walk with God.
- Don't worry, be happy.
- Put God first and follow the plan.

Promises to Cherish

Behold, I will do a new thing, now it shall spring forth; shall you not know it? I will even make a road in the wilderness and rivers in the desert. (Isaiah 43:19)

Do not remember the former things, nor consider the things of old. (Isaiah 43:18)

And God will wipe away every tear from their eyes; there shall be no more death, nor sorrow, nor crying. There shall be no more pain, for the former things have passed away. (Revelation 21:4)

I will bring the blind by a way they did not know; I will lead them in paths they have not known. I will make darkness light before them, and crooked places straight. These things I will do for them, and not forsake them. (Isaiah 42:16)

Today's Date_____

My Prayers

_____
_____
_____
_____
_____
_____
_____
_____
_____
_____
_____
_____
_____
_____
_____
_____
_____
_____
_____
_____
_____
_____
_____
_____
_____

Today's Date_____

My Answers

_____
_____
_____
_____
_____
_____
_____
_____
_____
_____
_____
_____
_____
_____
_____
_____
_____
_____
_____
_____
_____
_____
_____
_____
_____
_____
_____
_____
_____

Today's Date_____

My Thoughts

_____
_____
_____
_____
_____
_____
_____
_____
_____
_____
_____
_____
_____
_____
_____
_____
_____
_____
_____
_____
_____
_____
_____
_____
_____

CHAPTER SIX

Get the Future

GO GIRL!

Where will you go, Miss Muffet? Will you choose the way of the Lord? You have chosen the Lord as your God. Here is what He promises as you GET GOING:

And though the Lord gives you the bread of adversity and the water of affliction, yet your teachers will not be moved into a corner anymore, But your eyes shall see your teachers. Your ears shall hear a word behind you, saying, "this is the way, walk in it," Whenever you turn to the right hand Or whenever you turn to the left. (Isaiah 30:20-21)

And one more marvelous verse that confirms God's desire is to lead you and that He can actually lead you:

For if you live according to the flesh you will die; but if by the Spirit you put to death the deeds of the body, you will live. For as many as are led by the Spirit of God, these are sons of God. For you did not receive the spirit of bondage again to fear, but you received the Spirit of adoption by whom we cry out, "Abba, Father." (Romans 8:13-15)

The Soap Opera

- I am not sure I can do thIsaiah
- I am concerned I will forget to pray.
- I hope I don't give up.
- I am scared.

What Do I Want to Pray About?

_____

_____

_____

_____

_____

Take Action

1. Pray each day. Spend that valuable time with Him.
2. Set that new goal—one that is easy to accomplish.
3. Help someone this week.
4. Be encouraged. You're doing something!

The Cure

Now you are on the way to becoming the new you, regenerated and renewed by the grace of God. With God's grace you can be healed, live in His will, help others to do the same!

Miss Muffet's Workbench

What Is My Part?

Have some fun. You're already on the right track. Here are some things to do, that are easy for any of us:

Things To Do At Church

1. Women's ministry
2. Join the prayer ministry
3. Children's ministry
4. Volunteer at the church office
5. Help out with the food pantry
6. If you are a musician, get involved
7. Check out the Rapid Responders
8. Go to some of the extra events
9. Get involved in a small group if they have them
10. Inquire about what is going on at the church

Things To Do In Everyday Life

1. Go for a walk
2. Walk up and down a flight of stairs
3. Play tennis; play volleyball
4. Work out at a fitness center
5. Go to a park
6. Go for a drive with your family
7. Go to a movie
8. Go to the zoo
9. Go to a museum
10. Take a class

A friend in Bible college once told me he was never lonely because he always made plans. Very interesting. I heard him that day. Part of my trouble was the lack of plans. Hence I would get very lonely. Get involved!

What Is God's Part?

You will see God moving in your life. Of course you will. He is God. He is true and His Word is true. He doesn't lie. Be encouraged. He will give you all the grace you ask for and need. Note that in every place where prayer is mentioned, He says "ASK." He likes you to ask. Don't just assume. Don't just "turn it over to Him." Get some conversation going.

The Prayer

Dear God, I am asking You to put me on the right track. You are my salvation. Lord Jesus, You are the source of my life. Please do a new work on the inside of me. Change every part of me: my heart, my mind, and my paths. Work all things according to Your will and pleasure, in Jesus' name. Amen.

Think About It

He is moving in your life because you asked Him. He loves you, He cares for you. He is encouraging. His Word even says HE CAN DO NEW THINGS as we shared in a previous chapter. It definitely bears repeating:

> *Do not remember the former things, nor consider the things of old. Behold, I will do a new thing, now it shall spring forth; shall you not know it? I will even make a road in the wilderness and rivers in the desert. (Isaiah 43:18-19)*

Promises to Cherish

Now this is the confidence that we have in Him, that if we ask anything according to His will, He hears us. And if we know that He hears us, whatever we ask, we know that we have the petitions that we have asked of Him (1 John 5:14–15).

Behold, the former things have come to pass, Now I declare new things; Before they spring forth I proclaim them to you. (Isaiah 42:9)

You have heard; look at all thIsaiah And you, will you not declare it? I proclaim to you new things from this time, even hidden things which you have not known. (Isaiah 48:6)

How will they preach unless they are sent? Just as it is written, "How beautiful are the feet of those who bring good news of good things!" (Romans 10:15)

And He who sits on the throne said, "Behold, I am making all things new." And He said, "Write, for these words are faithful and true." (Revelation 21:5)

*Today's Date*_____

My Prayers

_____
_____
_____
_____
_____
_____
_____
_____
_____
_____
_____
_____
_____
_____
_____
_____
_____
_____
_____
_____
_____
_____
_____
_____

Today's Date_____

My Answers

_____
_____
_____
_____
_____
_____
_____
_____
_____
_____
_____
_____
_____
_____
_____
_____
_____
_____
_____
_____
_____
_____
_____
_____
_____

Today's Date_____

My Thoughts

Go Girl

TOOL KIT

CHAPTER SEVEN

Get the Antidote

PRAYER IS VITAL

Be sure and look at the section of notes about forgiveness, and research from medical universities showing that healing can occur through forgiveness.

Forgiving others is powerful. Receiving forgiveness is also powerful. Think about having a clear conscience and the peace of mind that it brings. God can give this to us. Good advice: Forgive, and be forgiven.

Keys to Successful Prayer

This chapter will give you the keys to experiencing results in prayer. It's not a matter of using a key to "get want you want." There is no selfishness involved. I use the word "key" because I found, to my joy, that making a few changes in how I prayed totally regenerated my prayer life and filled my heart and mind with peace.

Be anxious for nothing, but in everything by prayer and supplication, with thanksgiving, let your requests be made known to God; and the peace of God, which surpasses all understanding, will guard your hearts and minds through Christ Jesus. (Philippians 4:6–7)

The above verse is the theme Scripture for the teaching on prayer. From the apostle Paul we get this advice: Don't worry; instead, pray about everything. It then adds that the peace of God, which surpasses understanding, will keep our hearts and minds through Christ Jesus. What a promise! Of course, we must pray according to God's will and in line with what Scripture teaches us. But many things are God's will.

In the Old Testament, David prayed that God would overthrow and overturn the works of darkness, and in response God sent out His arrows and scattered the foe, lightnings in abundance, and He vanquished them (Psalm 18:14). There are many answers to personal prayers in the Bible. Have you ever wanted to pray but didn't know how to begin? Or have you tried everything but not received the joy and fulfillment you had hoped for in prayer?

Through these steps, you will become renewed in your excitement for spiritual things and about God Himself, His faithfulness, and the integrity of His Word.

The price Jesus paid for our sins at Calvary affords us the opportunity to be born again and to come into the family of God, which is the Christian's greatest gift. The relationship we can then have with our God is the next greatest gift.

Prayer is the key to building a close relationship with God. As you engage in prayer, you will never be the same again. Prayer need not be tedious. God does not require you to perform a list of prerequisites before He will answer you. Yet there are things that God asks of us.

Before You Start
Before you pray, you need to be sure there is nothing between you and God. You need to ask for forgiveness of your sins. You also need to forgive others of anything you have against them. How can we ask for forgiveness if we refuse to forgive others their trespasses against us (Luke 6:37 and 17:3)?

If I feel like I can't forgive, I ask for His help: "God, I can't forgive, but I ask You to love and forgive in and through me by Your Holy Spirit. Please give me the grace." This will work!

Leave your gift there before the altar, and go your way. First be reconciled to your brother, and then come and offer your gift. (Matt. 5:24)

Studies on Forgiveness
Stanford Medicine, Volume 16, Number 4, Summer 1999, published a quarterly by Stanford University Medical Center: *The Art and Science of Forgiveness.* "If you feel good but want to feel even better, try forgiving someone." —FREDERIC LUSKIN, PH.D. You can research this on the Stanford Medical Website to read it in its entirety.

Receiving Forgiveness
Forgiving others is powerful, according to the above study, and it brings emotional and physical benefits to your life. It also can benefit the lives of those being forgiven. Perhaps there can

now be the opportunity for healing in a once-severed relationship. Forgiveness gives us a clear conscience and the associated peace of mind. "Forgive and be forgiven" is good advice. "Let your requests be made known to God; and the peace of God, which surpasses all understanding, will guard your hearts and minds through Christ Jesus" Philippians 4:6–7.

Mini Prayer Workshop

Let's Get Started!

1. Confess and receive forgiveness for any sin, including unforgiveness, doubt, unbelief, fear, and anything else that might be between you and God (1 John 1:9).

2. List your requests. "Let your requests be made known to God" (Philippians 4:6).

3. Take authority over the enemy. Pray that God will "overthrow and overturn the works of darkness" (2 Chronicles 25:8).

4. Pray in detail. Make specific (scriptural) requests to the Father in Jesus' name. You can always add "if it be Your will" to the end of a prayer if you don't know the will of God.

5. Place your trust in His specific promises. Know that we rest our faith in who God is, in His integrity, and in the integrity of His Word.

6. Thank God and praise Him for what He is doing according to His will. "By prayer and supplication with thanksgiving, let your requests be made known to God" (Philippians 4:6).

What Is GOD'S Part?

God is faithful. His promises are true (1 Corinthians 1:20). His Word is true (Romans 3:4). He will watch over His Word to perform it (Isaiah 55:11). So, when you find promises upon which to rest your faith, God is pleased. He will hear and answer you. You must realize that God has more love and understanding for His creation than we can possibly comprehend. He is also more powerful than we can grasp.

Promises to Cherish

Be anxious for nothing, but in everything by prayer and supplication, with thanksgiving, let your requests be made known to God; and the peace of God, which surpasses all understanding, will guard your hearts and minds through Christ Jesus. (Philippians 4:6–7)

Whatever you ask in My name, that I will do, that the Father may be glorified in the Son. If you ask anything in My name, I will do it. (John 14:13–14)

Most assuredly, I say to you, whatever you ask the Father in My name He will give you. Until now you have asked nothing in My name. Ask, and you will receive, that your joy may be full. (John 16:23–24)

All the promises of God in Him are Yes, and in Him Amen, to the glory of God through us. (2 Corinthians 1:2)

Now to Him who is able to do exceedingly abundantly above all that we ask or think, according to the power that works in us, to Him be glory in the church by Christ Jesus to all generations, forever and ever. Amen. (Ephesians 3:20–21)

Today's Date_____

My Prayers

_____
_____
_____
_____
_____
_____
_____
_____
_____
_____
_____
_____
_____
_____
_____
_____
_____
_____
_____
_____
_____
_____

Today's Date_____

My Answers

_____
_____
_____
_____
_____
_____
_____
_____
_____
_____
_____
_____
_____
_____
_____
_____
_____
_____
_____
_____
_____
_____
_____
_____
_____
_____
_____
_____
_____

Today's Date_____

My Thoughts

_____
_____
_____
_____
_____
_____
_____
_____
_____
_____
_____
_____
_____
_____
_____
_____
_____
_____
_____
_____
_____
_____
_____

CHAPTER EIGHT

Prayer Promises

TO REMEMBER

Partakers of His Nature

His divine power has given to us all things that pertain to life and godliness, through the knowledge of Him who called us by glory and virtue, by which have been given to us exceedingly great and precious promises, that through these you may be partakers of the divine nature, having escaped the corruption that is in the world through lust. (2 Peter 1:3–4)

Abide in God

If you abide in Me, and My words abide in you, you will ask what you desire, and it shall be done for you. (John 15:7)

This Book of the Law shall not depart from your mouth, but you shall meditate in it day and night, that you may observe to do according to all that is written in it. For then you will make your way prosperous, and then you will have good success. (Joshua 1:8)

[We] *thank God without ceasing, because when you received the word of God which you heard from us, you welcomed it not as the word of men, but as it is in truth, the word of God, which also effectively works in you who believe.* (1 Thessalonians 2:13)

God Is Powerful
It is the Spirit who gives life; the flesh profits nothing. The words that I speak to you are spirit, and they are life. (John 6:63)

So shall My Word be that goes forth from My mouth; it shall not return to Me void, but it shall accomplish what I please, and it shall prosper in the thing for which I sent it. (Isaiah 55:11)

And what is the exceeding greatness of His power toward us who believe, according to the working of His mighty power which He worked in Christ when He raised Him from the dead... (Ephesians 1:19–20)

We are His workmanship, created in Christ Jesus for good works, which God prepared beforehand that we should walk in them. (Ephesians 2:10)

In Time of Trouble
He who has begun a good work in you will complete it until the day of Jesus Christ. (Philippians 1:6)

The Lord will deliver me from every evil work and preserve me for His heavenly kingdom. To Him be glory forever and ever. Amen! (2 Timothy 4:18)

For Protection

No evil shall befall you, nor shall any plague come near your dwelling; for He shall give His angels charge over you, to keep you in all your ways. (Psalm 91:10–1)

Promises for Answered Prayer

Be anxious for nothing, but in everything by prayer and supplication, with thanksgiving, let your requests be made known to God; and the peace of God, which surpasses all understanding, will guard your hearts and minds through Christ Jesus. (Philippians 4:6–7)

Whatever you ask in My name, that I will do, that the Father may be glorified in the Son. If you ask anything in My name, I will do it. (John 14:13–14)

Most assuredly, I say to you, whatever you ask the Father in My name He will give you. Until now you have asked nothing in My name. Ask, and you will receive, that your joy may be full. (John 16:23–24)

All the promises of God in Him are Yes, and in Him Amen, to the glory of God through us. (2 Corinthians 1:2)

Now to Him who is able to do exceedingly abundantly above all that we ask or think, according to the power that works in us, to Him be glory in the church by Christ Jesus to all generations, forever and ever. Amen. (Ephesians 3:20–21)

My God shall supply all your need according to His riches in glory by Christ Jesus. (Philippians 4:19)

This is the confidence that we have in Him, that if we ask anything according to His will, He hears us. And if we know that He hears us, whatever we ask, we know that we have the petitions that we have asked of Him. 1 (John 5:14–15)

Jesus's Words: Forgiveness; Prayer

When you pray, you shall not be like the hypocrites. For they love to pray standing in the synagogues and on the corners of the streets, that they may be seen by men. Assuredly, I say to you, they have their reward. But you, when you pray, go into your room, and when you have shut your door, pray to your Father who is in the secret place; and your Father who sees in secret will reward you openly. And when you pray, do not use vain repetitions as the heathen do. For they think that they will be heard for their many words. Therefore do not be like them. For your Father knows the things you have need of before you ask Him. In this manner, therefore, pray:

Our Father in heaven,
Hallowed be Your name.
Your kingdom come.
Your will be done
On earth as it is in heaven.
Give us this day our daily bread.
And forgive us our debts,
As we forgive our debtors.
And do not lead us into temptation,
But deliver us from the evil one.
For Yours is the kingdom and the power
and the glory forever. Amen.
For if you forgive men their trespasses,
your heavenly Father will also forgive you.
But if you do not forgive men their trespasses,
neither will your Father forgive your trespasses.
(Matthew 6:5–15)

Today's Date_____

My Prayers

_____
_____
_____
_____
_____
_____
_____
_____
_____
_____
_____
_____
_____
_____
_____
_____
_____
_____
_____
_____
_____
_____
_____
_____

*Today's Date*_____

My Answers

_____
_____
_____
_____
_____
_____
_____
_____
_____
_____
_____
_____
_____
_____
_____
_____
_____
_____
_____
_____
_____
_____
_____
_____
_____
_____
_____

*Today's Date*_____

My Thoughts

_____
_____
_____
_____
_____
_____
_____
_____
_____
_____
_____
_____
_____
_____
_____
_____
_____
_____
_____
_____
_____
_____
_____
_____
_____
_____
_____
_____

CHAPTER NINE

Forgiveness

RESEARCH & RESOURCES

These research projects study the effects of forgiveness on stress, happiness, coping with major illness, and more.

"Interpersonal Forgiveness: The Role of Cognitive Appraisal, Empathy & Humility"

Peter Hill, Ph.D., in the Department of Psychology at Grove City College, at the time of funding, and now at Biola University, Rosemead School of Psychology, will investigate an individual's right to decide to forgive or not to forgive (or seek forgiveness). The study consists of using a survey, interviews, and workshops to help evaluate the measures of stress reduction. The objectives include understanding how different people have differing perceptions of wrongdoing, experiencing empathy towards the other person, and being more able to request and offer forgiveness.

"Psychosocial Effects of Forgiveness Training with Adults"

Carl Thoresen, Ph.D., professor of psychology at Stanford University, will study methods of helping people forgive in order to reduce hostility and anger toward their offenders. Thoresen believes that people who replace anger, hostility, and hatred with forgiveness will have better cardiovascular health and fewer long-term health problems. This project uses assessments, interviews, and group sessions. The study will incorporate men and women as a means to study if gender differences exist in forgiveness and if so, to clarify those differences. Thoresen's project was directed by Dr. Fred Luskin.

Mayo Clinic:
Forgiveness: Letting go of grudges and bitterness

When someone you care about hurts you, you can hold on to anger, resentment and thoughts of revenge — or embrace forgiveness and move forward.

http://www.mayoclinic.com/health/forgiveness/mh00131

Here, Katherine Piderman, Ph.D., staff chaplain at Mayo Clinic, Rochester, Minn., discusses forgiveness and how it can lead you down the path of physical, emotional and spiritual well-being.

Forgiveness in Health Research and Medical Practice:
http://www.explorejournal.com/article/S15508307%2805%2
900154-0/abstract

Everett L. Worthington Jr, PhD1; Charlotte vanOyen Witvliet, PhD2; Andrea J. Lerner, BS1; Michael Scherer, MS1:

In this issue, Worthington, Witvliet, Lerner, and Scherer discuss how forgiveness is taking its place as an important issue in healthcare.

Many readers of EXPLORE may not realize that "forgiveness research" even exists. The field is indeed new, but, over the past decade, it has grown exponentially and is maturing admirably. We now know that there is not just a psychology underlying forgiveness but a physiology as well.

Forgiveness is an ancient concept. It is enshrined in all the great religions as a gesture of supreme value. It is a mark of compassion, love, and caring—and is thus a natural concern of the healing professions, whose essence embodies these very qualities.

There are no boundaries to forgiveness. Although Worthington et al focus on the importance of forgiveness within and between individuals, forgiveness is also being discussed at national and international levels. Should creditor nations forgive third-world debt? Should those who have been enslaved forgive their oppressors? Should victims of holocausts forgive their tormentors? Can we summon the humility that is required to seek forgiveness for our attempted genocide of native peoples? For degrading our environment, the only home we have?

A society that cannot forgive is one without a heart. We should not wish to live in such a society—or a world— in which forgiveness is never extended. With the escalating religious and political hatreds around the world, and the increasingly sinister ways of seeking vengeance, it is uncertain whether a civilization that is devoid of forgiveness can continue to exist.

These considerations exceed the concerns of Worthington et al, but they follow naturally from their findings. These authors and the forgiveness researchers they cite are onto something exceedingly important, something that is essential not just to our welfare but to our survival as well.

—Larry Dossey, MD
Executive Editor, EXPLORE

Freeing Myself Through Forgiveness
by Yolanda Young

http://www.npr.org/templates/story/story.php?storyId=14547176&ps=rs

Yolanda Young is a lawyer in Washington, D.C., and author of the book and syndicated column, "On Our Way to Beautiful." She previously worked for the National Football League Players' Association. Young is on the board of the PEN/Faulkner Foundation.

Stanford Medical University Study
Stanford Medicine, Volume 16, Number 4, Summer 1999, which is published quarterly by Stanford University Medical Center:

The Art and Science of Forgiveness
If you feel good but want to feel even better, try forgiving someone. —FREDERIC LUSKIN, PH.D.

For centuries, the world's religious and spiritual traditions have recommended the use of forgiveness as a balm for hurt or angry feelings. Psychotherapists have worked to help their clients to forgive, and some have written about the importance of forgiveness. Until recently, however, the scientific literature has not had much to say about the effect of forgiveness. But that's starting to change. While the scientific study of forgiveness is just beginning—the relevant intervention research having been conducted only during the past ten years—when taken together, the work so far demonstrates the power of forgiveness to heal emotional wounds and hints that forgiveness may play a role in physical healing as well. What is intriguing about this research is that even people who are not depressed or particularly anxious can obtain the improved emotional and psychological functioning that comes from learning to forgive. This suggests that forgiveness may enable people who are functioning adequately to feel even better. Published studies on forgiveness have shown the importance of forgiveness training on coping with a variety of psychologically painful experiences.

Studies have been conducted with adolescents who felt neglected by their parents, with women who were abused as children, with elderly women who felt hurt or uncared for, with males who disagreed with their female partners' decisions to have abortions and with college students who had been hurt.

These studies showed that when given forgiveness training of varying lengths and intensities, participants could become less hurt and become more able to forgive their offenders.

Forgiveness heals the heart, research hints

May 20, 1999: Web posted at: 4:00 p.m. EDT (2000 GMT)

From Medical Correspondent Eileen O'Connor

WASHINGTON (CNN) -- Littleton. Kosovo. Now Georgia. Never before, say some experts, has there been such a need to forgive what seems to be the unforgivable.

Studies funded by the Templeton Forgiveness Research Campaign are trying to monitor and measure the physiological effects of forgiveness and its benefits, taken from the pulpit into the lab.

Everett Worthington is the director of the campaign. One day after mailing off his manuscript outlining a step-by-step process of forgiveness, his own ability was sorely tested when his mother was murdered.

http://www.cnn.com/HEALTH/9905/20/forgiveness/

CHAPTER TEN

My Prayer

JOURNAL

I want you to start a Prayer Journal. Put in your requests, and note when the Lord answers, as HE DOES answer. It will definitely encourage you. PLUS it will help you have faith.

Things to Remember

1. God *can* do a new thing. He is not limited.

2. He is there for you.

3. God loves you. Your relationship with God is your greatest gift. Nurture it. It will grow.

4. All you are and can be comes from your life in Jesus Christ. Draw near to Him.

    Walk with Him. Talk with Him. Philippians 4:19 says that God will provide all of your needs according to His riches in glory by Christ Jesus.

*Today's Date*_____

My Prayers

_____
_____
_____
_____
_____
_____
_____
_____
_____
_____
_____
_____
_____
_____
_____
_____
_____
_____
_____
_____
_____
_____
_____
_____

Today's Date_____

My Answers

_____
_____
_____
_____
_____
_____
_____
_____
_____
_____
_____
_____
_____
_____
_____
_____
_____
_____
_____
_____
_____
_____
_____
_____
_____
_____
_____

My Thoughts

Today's Date_____

_____
_____
_____
_____
_____
_____
_____
_____
_____
_____
_____
_____
_____
_____
_____
_____
_____
_____
_____
_____
_____
_____
_____
_____
_____
_____